Arts and Crafts

IN

INDONESIA

THE INDONESIAN COMMITTEE
OF
THE NEW YORK WORLD'S FAIR
1964-1965

Introduction

From time immemorial arts and crafts have been exercised by the people of Indonesia. Each island, even each region has almost its own method and way of expressing them. The sense of art of the people finds an extensive field of work in the making of objects of daily use. Originally everybody made what was required for daily use. Having much time at their disposal and the certainty that the object would be of great use, was the reason for taking so much pain in the making of these objects. Even the most simple object became a product of the maker's ingenuity and artistic sense. He made his object not with the set purpose to become famous, but merely because he loved his work.

However, the closer contact with the outerworld, the increase of trade, the import of European and American manufactured articles etc. have brought upon a great change in the field of arts and crafts too. The use of aniline dyes, the copying of modern designs from various imported women magazines, the remodelling of the articles of use, unmistakably refer to modern influences from the western countries. Our artists and craftsmen of nowadays earn their living with the products of their hands. They are now concerned with a nationwide recognition.

But even so, there is still much preserved in different parts of Indonesia. Japara, Jogjakarta and Surakarta in Central Java are still centres of many classic arts and crafts as well as the wonderful island of Bali. In South and Central Sulawesi, in the Padang Highlands, the land of the Minangkabau, the Lampongs and Palembang in southern Sumatra, and on the islands of Nusa Tenggara, the former lesser Sunda Islands (Bali, Lombok, Sumbawa, Flores, Timor, Sumba, Roti and Savu) and in the Moluccas the art of fine weaving is still exercised, though much is now done with imported chemicals and articifial silk threads.

3

The hand-made batik is at present but restricted to a very small group of batik-artists. It is more and more replaced by the so-called batik-tjap or printing-methods.

The art of painting is mainly adopted from the West. Traditional painting nowadays exists in Bali only, where the Balinese painters have remained faithfully to the way of painting they have inherited from their ancestors and where this graphic art is still exercised by nearly all Balinese painters.

Indonesia with her more than 3,000 islands has such a vast variety of arts and crafts that it is highly interesting to know something about them.

At exhibitions an attempt is made to show the visitors as many products as possible of our arts and crafts which might attract the attention. But it should be wrong to draw the conclusion from the exhibits that there is nothing more to see in our country itself. In fact much more is to be seen and to be admired. The natural environs in which they work enhance the romantic atmosphere and make the visitor think how it could be possible to create such a work of high artistic value with such simple materials and very often, under such primitive circumstances. Besides our musea, spread over the whole of Indonesia, are storehouses of the highest interest and beauty.

May this booklet find its way to the bookcases of our many, many friends abroad.

DJAKARTA, January 1964

THE INDONESIAN COMMITTEE
OF
THE NEW YORK WORLD'S FAIR
1964-1965

INDONESIAN ORNAMENTAL DESIGNS

GEOMETRICAL FIGURES

 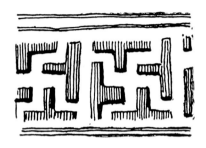

Tumpuls

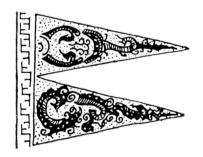 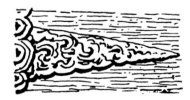

INDONESIAN ORNAMENTAL DESIGNS

It goes without saying that each country has its own specific ornamental designs, depicted from its own natural environs and from its own national life. The various tribes of each country too has respectively preserved their own tribal designs and in countries where formerly feudal families were in power, each family had their own totem, which was applied in the various articles of art, dress etc. There were also artists who just made the figures without having any particular in mind. So in judging the patterns of a particular article, we need not always think of some deep and mystical idea connected with it.

The most widely spread design here in Indonesia is the geometrical ornament. It is the outcome of a technical factor. The geometrical ornament is clearly seen in plaiting. The strips are simply interwoven. When it is once up and down, then the pattern results in squares. And when it is once up and twice down, then the outcome is a twill pattern that can be applied in various ways. This geometrical ornament is also seen in earthenware. Even in the late stone period we already find simple geometrical ornamentation. Usually this ornamentation is scratched into the clay, when it is still soft. Of course, in weaving too this same pattern is very much used. It is determined by the technique itself as in the case of plaiting. If in the cloth, for the warp or for the woof, groups of threads of different colours are used, then a striped cloth is obtained. If the same is done for the warp and the woof simultaneously, then the result is a diamond pattern. This simple ornamention is found throughout the archipelago.

Special mention should be made of the geometrical ornament in the so-called "tumpal". A tumpal-border consists of a row of isosceles triangles.

In Hindu-Javanese architecture we also find the tumpal-decoration, which is sometimes very handsomely elaborated. A fine example of this is to be seen at the Naga or Snake temple near Blitar in East Java.

But this tumpal-decoration is best-known in the textile and batik-art. In the woven "sarong" as well as in the "kain batik" we find a broad strip across the cloth. This strip is called "kapala" (head) and is ornamented with two rows of tumpals whose tips approach each other. The tumpals themselves are ornamented with flower motifs.

In the so-called "kain songket" (made in Palembang and Bali) the tumpal-motif is generally found. In these cloths the ornament is not batiked on, but it is woven into with a gold thread.

Varieties of geometrical designs: The principal motif of these varieties is that of squares with semi-circles along the four sides. In the art of the Torajas (Central Sulawesi) the geometrical design is widely spread and has great significance. The so-called "kawung" motif in the batik is based on a geometrical design. It mainly consists of circles placed in a row so that they partly overlap one another. This "kawung" motif is the "djalamprang" pattern, whose basic form also consists of circles placed in a row; only with this difference that the circles do not partly overlap, but they merely touch one another. The circles are filled up with rosettes and other figures. This basic form is also found on the clothing of old stone or bronze Hindu-Javanese statues.

Geometrical Ornament (Double Spiral): Throughout Indonesia the double spiral design is familiar. It has the shape of an S. It came here with the bronze culture, which is also known in the Allied European bronze culture. This double spiral motif has penetrated far into the eastern part of the archipelago, even into West Irian, especially along the north coast, where it evidently arrived, as it did in other parts of Indonesia, together with the bronze or Dong Son culture. For in northern West Irian we also find the bronze hatches and other bronze objects of that culture.

Double spiral designs were also used to ornament tree-bark in olden times. The bark of several kinds of trees was formerly beaten and worked up into articles of clothing in many parts of Indonesia. The decoration of the beaten bark, however, develped into an art in two regions only: Central Sulawesi (Torajas) and northern West Irian.

Double spiral and "parang rusak";

One of the best-known batik-designs is the so-called "parang rusak", which occurs in various forms. Was it formerly worn by the nobility, at present it has become very popular. There might be a possible relation between the double spiral and the "parang rusak" motif, as it is quite possible that the double spiral motif from the bronze period has had some influence upon it, especially on the manner in which the spaces are filled up.

8

A tumpal-decoration with geometrical figures on a kain batik.

A beautifully carved Toraja-house, where the various ornamental designs are clearly visible. Mind also the decorative motifs on the skirts of the girls.

DOUBLE SPIRALS

Hooks

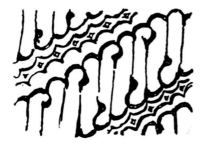

Parang Rusak

Cloud-boraer

Meander: In the bronze period a group of designs came to Indonesia from South-east Asia, which, in the art of batik is collectively referred to as "bandji" ornamentation. They also occur in the Chinese art. One of the best-known is the "meander" in various shapes, which are also known in the old Greek art designes and which therefore is also sometimes called "Greek Frieze". When the corners are rounded off, the result is again a border of concatenated double spirals, dating from the bronze age.

The meander-border is also found in another form, both in European and in East Asiatic art. It can be described as a series of "T"'s, alternatively upright and upside down. This form is quite general in Chinese art and it has come to Indonesia in this shape. Such a motif does not always signify a cloud-border; in the Hindu art of East Java it is also used to indicate the edge of a garment and it also found in European art. Especially in the Cheribon area this cloud-border motif is widely spread.

Amongst the so-called "bandji" -designs the swastika is one of the most important, together with the hook and key designs. The swastika is especially referred to as "bandji" in Chinese. In the bronze period this swastika was also quite general in Europe, symbolizing the rotation of the celestial bodies, and is more especially the symbol of the sun, until it became a sign of luck in general. In Indonesia this ornamental design usually occurs as part of a space-filling, the remainder of which consists of rectilinear figures, both referred to as "bandji". The "bandji" motifs (swastika and meander) are related to the so-called hook or key-designs. They may be regarded as legs of the swastika or hooks of the meander, used separately and placed in rows or arranged otherwise. The motif, on account of its rectangular form, is especially appropriate for weaving and matting.

"Wall-paper"-patterns: Various geometrical and semi-geometrical ornamental designs, still applied in the art of batik, were already applied in Hindu-Javanese architecture, serving as decorations on rectangular spaces on the outerwalls of temples. They are sometimes called "wall-paper patterns", because of their close resemblance and wall-paper is used to decorate bare wall-spaces (see Tjandi Prambanan near Jogja). The same eight leaved rosette which we find on the wall of Tjandi Prambanan a thousand years old, also occur in various woven cloths, more especially in the songkets (Palembang and Bali).

11

The Human Body: The human body as a motif of art-design is already found in prehistoric and primitive ornamentation. In the old symbolic art of Indonesia the human body represents two ideas: protection against evil, and the depiction of ancestors, which is also more or less protective. To the primitive mind the symbol is not merely a representation, but it has also the magical force of what is depicted. Thus the representation of a human being has the magical force of that human being, and in this way the human figure can have a protective effect (Kalimantan, Sumba etc.). The heft of a kris (kind of a dagger), especially before the introduction of the Islam, was often a squatting human figure, sometimes with a bird's head.

The Mask: It is not only the entire human body that is used in ornamentation; we also find separate parts, especially those exercising the greatest magical power, primarily the face (mask) and the eyes. The mask serves as a protection against evil. In Hindu-Indonesian art the mask occurs very frequently. In India it is often taken for a lion's head; but in Indonesia it merges into a human face, especially a demon's head, a "kala"-figure. In the Hindu art of Central Java the mask in such cases is often represented without the lower jaw, but in East Java and Bali with the lower jaw. The mask (a kalafigure) is often found over a temple entrance.

Wayang: Wayang figures are used in great superfluity in modern Indonesian arts and crafts. But this is not something of this time, for wayang figures already occurred in the ancient ornamental art repeatedly. Characters from the Ramayana epic are often depicted. They were naturally first applied in temples, dating from the 13th century, çaka (the çaka era begins with the year 78 A.D.)

Old Javanese weapons, especially the kris, occasionally have wayang figures wrought in the blade. This need not surprise us, in view of the magical significance of the kris. On articles of cast brass wayang figures are also often found. In Bali various articles of coconut-shells are painted with wayang figures, which is also the case with paintings on cloth, on wood etc.

The buffalo: The ancestors of the Indonesians knew the buffalo as a domestic animal as early as in the late stone age (neolithicum) and they worshipped it as a sacred animal. That's why up to very day the motif of the buffalo's head is to be found as a symbol

12

THE HUMAN BODY

The Buffalo

The Mask

of the fertile earth, and as a protection against evil. By the shape
of its horns the buffalo is related to the moon. The buffalo's
head is used as a decoration of the front of houses in the Batak
and in the Toraja-lands.

Other animals which are often used as decorations are the elephant,
the horse, the lion, the winged lion, the stag, the makara. This
is an imaginary animal, having the shape of a fish and the trunk
of an elephant; it resembles the dolphin in European art. This
makara motif came to Indonesia with the Hindu culture.

The bird: Throughout the world the bird plays an important role
as symbol and as ornament, and this is also the case in Indonesia.
The bird often symbolizes the soul of the deceased. The hornbill
is often used as a decoration among various Dayak-tribes. It
is the symbol of death and resurrection and to some Dayak tribes
it is also the symbol of the god of the upper-world.

The cock or rooster in European symbology is related to the sun,
because he crows about the hour of sunrise. In Indonesia too
this bird has more or less the same meaning. Besides that it
may also be a symbol of force, courage and fertility. In the
economic life the cock plays an important part in the cock-fights.
In the sacrified rites much use is made of cocks. Therefore it
stands to reason that it is repeatedly met in ornamentation. (Sumba
cloths, Palembang cloths etc.) Special mention should be made
of the garuda. In Hindu mythology this bird is the mount of
Vishnu. We often find this bird, in Hindu-Javanese art either together with Vishnu or without him. In Indonesia the garuda
is also the sunbird or the sun-eagle, and as such opposed to the
snake which symbolizes the waters and the under world. The
Coat of Arms of the Republic of Indonesia is the Garuda and
our Indonesian Airways too has the Garuda as its symbol. It
is the ornament for decorative lamps, and more especially for the
wayang lamp (blengtjong).

Naturally it is also a much beloved design of the batik. Sometimes the entire bird is a batik pattern, sometimes only its wings, or
even a single wing. In the batik art the wing pattern is called "lar".
The peacock, the parrot, the phoenix (imported from China),
the snake are very often used and which is also often referred to
as "naga" dragon.

The group of lower animals: The group of lower animals is represented by the crocodile, tortoise, lizard, iguana, shrimp, lobster,

14

shell etc. Scenes from Indonesian fables are often depicted in various articles of arts and crafts. The "kantjil", tragulus konchil takes a very important place in these. Flowers, leaves, buds and other vegetables have inspired our artists and craftsmen from time immemorial.

Here are some of the most applied patterns on batik: hooks, circles, square, keys, birds, flowers etc. Colours are more and more used now in order to meet the demands of the prevailing fashion.

A Parang pattern.

16

PLAITING WORK

PLAITING WORK

The making of baskets, the weaving of mats and more especially that of sleeping-mats, the wattling of fences, all this sort of handicraft is well-known over the whole of Indonesia. Gradually it developed into an art of its own. It offered a welcome opportunity to apply geometrical flat-ornaments in its most decorative complication.

It is a necessity in the house, in the field and even for the clothing. The indispensable basket-work had to be made according to a certain method and to a considerable measure of patience, it had to be plaited with concentration of thought and deliberation. Large baskets, bamboo-fences, house-walls etc. are made by the men, while the women keep themselves busy with the lighter type of baskets etc.

The surroundings of a village provide the materials for some house industry. Bamboo is widely spread and almost everywhere in Indonesia bamboo-groves are found. There are several kinds of bamboo. Some of them are not suitable for house-building. They can only be used for the making of all sorts of household articles. Young bamboos are cut down, soaked in water, dried and thin layers are cut out for the making of small articles, such as fans, tobacco-pouches, mats for wall-decoration etc. Bamboo-hats are also made of split bamboo. Older bamboo is the material for plaited walls and floors and for numerous kitchen-utensils. In the Minangkabau e.g. most of these articles are coloured and simple patterns inserted so that they look very attractive.

Bamboo is more widely spread in Java and Madura, Bali and Lombok. In Kalimantan, Sulawesi (the Celebes) and Sumatra rattan grows in abundance. Pandan-trees (Pandanacaea) grow in swampy places. Their leaves are dried and made suitable for baskets and mats. They are to be found in Java and Sumatra.

Bali:
hats, bags and fans of dried pandan leaves.

20

Hats for schoolgirls are made of dried pandan-leaves (*Tasikmalaja*).

Kalimantan women making food-covers of dried pandan-leaves with decorations.

Various articles made of orchid-fibres, South Sulawesi.

A Timorese hat of
dried pandanus-leaves. (lontar palm).
It is highly decorative.

The simplest use of a dried
pandanus-leaf: a scoop
for water. (lontarpalm)

As a sound-bottom for a musical instrument. It is known as sasando in Timor.

Floormats made of dried straw called mendong (fimbristylis efoliata stend, belonging to the Cypereaecae). They are made in the environs of Tasikmalaja.

A special sort of pandanus (lontarpalm, Borassas flabelliforums) grows on dry grounds. Large groves are to be found in Sulawesi and in the islands of Nusatenggara (the Lesser Sunda islands). Its leaves are fan-like and the people make all kinds of tings of them. In Timor they even make a sound-bottom for their musical instruments. It is called sasando. Its simple use is that for catching water from the well. But the people of South Sulawesi make most artistic little baskets and trays of these dried leaves of the pandanus. In Timor, Flores and Roti decorative hats for men are also made of this material.

In the environs of Bone, South Sulawesi, a very peculair kind of orchid with long leaves grows there. The people make the finest plaiting-work of these orchid-fibres.

Sisal is obtained from the leaves of the agave-plants. But for rope, it is also very suitable for simpler articles like dish and glass-covers, small carpets and bags.

The above-mentioned crafts are house-and village-industries. Co-operatives operate in these cases to collect the products and to sell them to several shops in town.

The baskets of the Minangkabau Highlands, the ones of Palembang with strong Chinese influence, those of Bali and Lombok and the ones of South Sulawesi show distinct varieties as a result of the different methods known to the plaiters.

The materials are easy to be had. The people prepare them by themselves or they buy them for little money. The work does not demand the whole time of the women. It can be done after the cooking. In this way they are able to earn some extra to add to the family-budget. Along the whole length of the village-street of Bona, centre of basket-works in South-Bali, girls, women and even children are seen plaiting: bags, fans, baskets, even sandals.

Research-work carried out in this field pointed out that it is one of the oldest house-industries in the tropics.

THE ART OF WEAVING

The weaving of kain pelangi,
Bali (pelangi = rainbow).

This woman binds (ikat) threads to be woven with different colours, Flores.

How did weaving come to Indonesia? Since time immemorial different weavings have been introduced into the archipelago from India. The European textile industry had also had much influence but not always a favourable one, because, with the import of cheap yerns and cottons, the quality of the woven products has gone down and in some places weaving has died out altogether. The Hindu influence, however, has left a lasting character in the technique and the design.

A Balinese woman working at her loom.

Judging from the primitive looms which are still to be found in the various places and the genuine native names they are called, there are indications that the art is one of the oldest properties of the Malay-Polynesian races. Even before the arrival of the Hindus in Indonesia weaving had already undergone influences from other countries. The human designs may originate from Chaldaea and outside Java and Madura where the people weave their own clothes, and there is a strict

Ikat-weavers on the island of Savu.

distinction between clothes for everyday use and festivals.

Four main types of weaving are known here: 1. ordinary cotton weaving; 2. silk weaving; 3. gold and silver thread weaving and 4. ikat weaving.

Weaving in Indonesia has not yet reached an industrial stage with rational labour divisions, but has remained an individual handicraft, and thus the articles are much more artistic. The weaver never shrinks from her primitive tools even though the labour is hard and long. What

31

These young girls are dressed for the Gending Criwijaya-dance.
Their head-covers are made of gold, their dresses are interwoven with gold threads. (Palembang, South Sumatra).

← An example of a songket Palembang richly interwoven with gold.

Young ladies of Kota Gedang, Central Sumatra, in their traditional festive attires. Gold is an essential part of the fabrics they wear.

her tools cannot achieve, her fingers can!

The art of weaving exhibits a great artistic taste in the producing of many-coloured fabrics. To achieve this effect, before proceeding to weaving, the threads are dyed in such a way that each thread acquires the desired colour over a definite length that is to be interwoven at a certain place in the cloth to be made. This is done by steeping the threads in the dye according to a saving-process bearing the name of "ikat". The word "ikat" means to bind or wrap and it is applied in weaving to a special method. The threads to be woven are first, before being dyed, bound or wrapped with "agel", a vegetable rope. In some parts only the thread for the warp undergoes this process and in other places only the woof thread, and a third method is to treat them both a like. In other words "ikat" is a binding or wrapping of yarns according to a certain design. This design comes to the fore in vague shapes after the yarns have been woven into one another. So the coloured pattern is prepared before the weaving is done.

For this purpose the weaver must have the pattern in her head precisely. She must know exactly which threads (in bundles) must absorb the dye and which not. The latter are then wrapped around with vegetable fibres (agel) which do not allow the dye to penetrate. These ikat-fibres also exhibit a rich variety in colour and ornamentation. Each district has its own pattern. Sometimes it is derived from the figures of their family-totem.

Starting with the darkest colour, those bindings (ikat) are removed after each steeping where the following colour should be brought upon and continued as long as all the desired colours have been used.

Now the weaving can be commenced, at which a neutral colour in the waft is kept. As a rule blue is the ground-colour and by using red for the second steeping, the warm tint is obtained, which is characteristic to this kind of weaving.

The cloths from Atjeh are dark red, often interwoven with silver or gold wire, the Balinese in cheerful colours with much yellow, the red decorative of Sumba cloths are among the best in the eastern part of Indonesia.

The Silungkang, Palembang and Lampong-weavings are rich in gold and silver ornamentation that they truly remind of the glorious era of Criwijaya.

THE ART OF BATIK

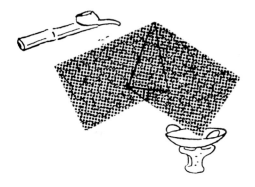

THE ART OF BATIK

Batik is almost restricted to Java. It is a free, individual art. The printing-technique is, being a mechanic work, bound to rules and patterns. The original starch- or wax-drop technique, imported by Persians or Egyptians from the remotest ages, amplified and improved by the Javanese, has been artistically improved by the Hindus. At any case, it must have been commenced with the most primitive dropping-method. The stem "tik" in the word "batik" means "a little bit", "a little dot", "a drop". That stem is to be traced in the Javanese word "tritik" or "taritik", a cloth on which appears a drawing which seems to be composed of drops. It is also found in the name "nitik" for the batik-pattern, imitating in dots a weaving-pattern. So the word "ambatik" may be literally translated as "(acloth) of drops (of wax or starch)."

Before the import of European piece-goods the cotton cloth had to be woven in the country itself. But this natural rough fibre, the so-called "kain kental", is not so very suitable for the fine drawing. Refinements came into existence on fine, thin, smooth material, so that the import of this fabricated material has had its benefit.

The white batik-material is generally called by the Javanese "muslim" or "mori", which is probably a corruption of "mousseline". It is first submitted to a preliminary treatment, serving to prevent the wax from penetrating too deeply into the woven material and to make this latter suitable for the penetration of the dye. As a means of prevention,

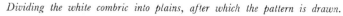

Dividing the white combric into plains, after which the pattern is drawn.

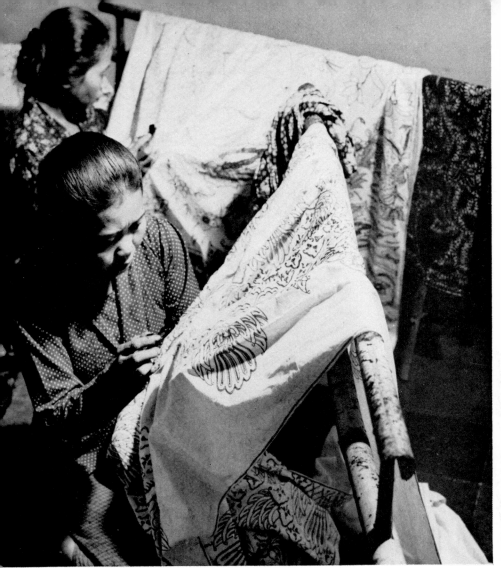

The drawing of the pattern with a tjanting.

Some isèn patterns.

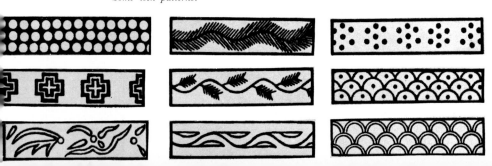

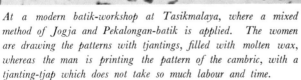

At a modern batik-workshop at Tasikmalaya, where a mixed method of Jogja and Pekalongan-batik is applied. The women are drawing the patterns with tjantings, filled with molten wax, whereas the man is printing the pattern of the cambric, with a tjanting-tjap which does not take so much labour and time.

starch is at present only used as an exception, wax is more and more used now. To introduce this substance the tjanting is used, a small sheet copper reservoir with more spouts, all according as to whether the batik-artist is to draw one or more parallel lines. A stove is beside her, upon which is a pan containing liquid wax. In front of her is the cloth to be treated, fixed upon a wooden frame. The outlines of the figures are first smeared over with wax: the spaces to be omitted are then filled with wax on both sides, and the sketch is ready. Then comes the filling of the sketch with all sorts of little ornaments, giving a livelier impression to the drawing and remaining within the contour-lines of a figure. This "filling" is generally called "isen".

A parang seling-pattern.

Fruit and flowers are often taken in conventionalized forms.

The first colour to be given to the batik is the blue or indigo. This appears in hundreds of nuances. The intensity of the colour depends on the way in which the very old colouring-process is applied. This blue colouring has become a profession and is generally done by men. Afterwards the cloth is washed, dried and the wax scratched off from

40

A galaran romo-pattern.

parts upon which the following colour has to be introduced, while the blue coloured patterns that have to remain blue, in their turn, are provided with a layer of wax. Before the introduction of the second dye is proceeded with, the thick layer of wax is broken here and there by the pinching. The result is that the new colour works its way in the cracks and a certain marble effect is produced. After the introduction of the new colour, if the design is completely carried out by this, the cloth is submitted to a further treatment to fix the colours.

All this handling takes much time. For the dyeing of a somewhat simple "kain" a period of about 40 days is required. The proper technique in batik is quite as difficult as that of etching or painting. It must be realized that this technique involves even surer understanding of line and colour, for it is practically impossible to correct a mistake in the drawing once it has been made, and it is also very nearly impossible to correct a mistake in colour.

41

An ancient pattern from Lasem.

42

As to the patterns, two main groups are to be distinguished: the one with geometrical desings, the other with more or less fantastic ornamentation. In the former the Indonesian ornamental forms are found, the latter is based upon Hindu designs.

Every district has its own peculiar colours and designs, each pattern has its own name. The batik-Jogja, batik-Solo and batik-Pekalongan are the best-known.

However, the increasing import of cheap fabrics, the rising standard of living makes that handmade batik has become too high in price for the average man and woman. In order to produce cheaper kains the tjap was invented. The tiap is a wooden block which has been set into the end of the grain small copper strips. These strips are carefully bent with tiny pilers until they assume the desered curves and are then fastened into the wood block. For the application of the wax, the tjaps are made in pairs, one for each side of the material. The process consists of dipping the block into the molten wax, touching the block to a pad to remove the excess wax, and then printing the wax on the material, after which the process is repeated with exactly as in the case of real batik. In this way the fine drawing with wax from the spout of the tjanting is avoided. Hence this batik-tjap is much cheaper, because it

Kain-kebaya for the svening.

An Indonesian creation of a batik dress.

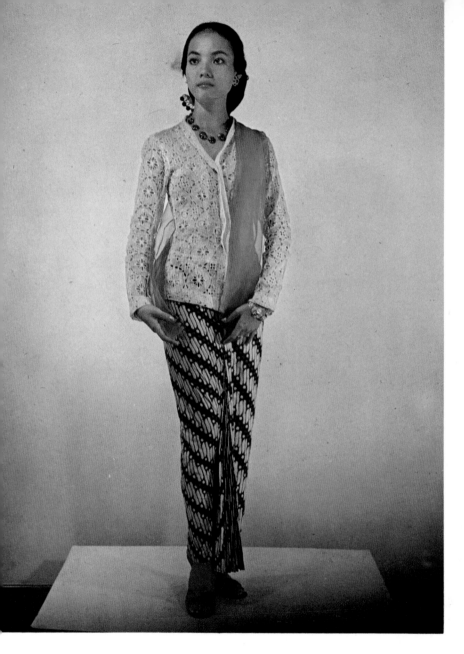

Kain-kebaya for special occasions.

Batik-Pekalongan with floral and bird-patterns in vivid colours.

Charming batik-sellers at the market of Solo.

has become a mass-production. To the layman there is hardly any differenc between a handmade and a tjap-batik but for the price. Another indication is the precise accuracy with which the figures are printed, while the handmade batik shows some irregularity of figures according to the skill of the batik-artist.

Indonesian creation of different kinds of batik dresses.

WOOD CARVING

WOOD CARVING

The presence of extensive forests with so many sorts of wood is one of the reasons why wood is so much used not only for building houses, the making of furniture and the like but it is also applied for finer crafts. In Central and West Java, and *Bali* the people make gamelan musical instruments which they decorate with beautiful carvings. Japara, a little town on the north coast of Java, is famous for its furniture and fancy-articles, while the Priangan has its dolls, wayang-golek, for their doll's theatres. The Minangkabau and the Bataks of North Sumatra and the Torajas of Central Sulawesi have houses all carved with characteristic figures. The

Making boxes with fine carvings (C. Jova).

Another piece of Balinese Woodcarving

The Garuda (Eagle), huge mystic bird of Hindu legend, a favourite mount of Vishnu

←*A Balinese artist working on a piece of statue.*

← Beautifully carved pillars

The Madurese too are
clever woodcarvers. This
exclusively ladies' writing-
desk is entirely carved.

*Burnt bamboo often used as
knitting-case (Toraja).*

front and side-walls of the Minangkabau house has fret-work orna-
mentations, often intensified by black, red and white colours. They
are decorated with leaf- and flower-motifs interlaced with claspers
and tendrils, showing a strong Hindu influence. The Bataks build
wooden houses and the façade has ingenious carving with the spiral
motif dominating.

The central figure is a representation of a buffalo's head serving
to ward off evil spirits. Which is also the case with the Toraja-houses.
In all these areas such houses are called Adat-houses in contrast to
the ordinary houses throughout Indonesia. The wooden façade of
a Toraja-house is abundantly ornamented with coloured carvings.
Then there is Bali with her countless statues of animals, people, temples,
birds, etc. etc. To think that most Indonesian artisans still use primitive
tools such as axes, compasses, saws, planes, hammers, files, drills and
gimlets, squares and that the final products can be so fine and exotic,
it is but natural that you'll get curious to see them work. The kinds
of wood used for this purpose are teak, iron-wood and striped ebony.

*A modern piece with decorative
wood-carving from Jogja.*

Specimens of the Sundanese Wayang Golek.

p. 64: The hero Arjuna and his spouse Sri Kandi. Mind their sarongs (skirts): Arjuna (left) has the Parang-rusak, whereas Sri Kandi (right) has the Kawun-motif.

SCULPTURE

SCULPTURE

The carving of stone has been known from the earliest possible time, since stone is everywhere to be found. With the arrival of the Hindus in Indonesia and by the time that some Indonesian sovereigns had embraced the Hindu religion and ordered some Hindu temples to be built, the people of various parts of Indonesia came to know this

A relief on the Hindu-Buddhist Borobudur near Magelang, Central Java. It depicts the life of Buddha, when he was still Prince Gautama.

art. And art being the permanent and sublime expression of the creative power inherent in a nation's character, it stands to reason that all elements which are to form this character, such as social organization, cultural pattern, religion, ideology, outside influences or lack of them, prosperity or decay, are bound to have an effect upon its art-

The wonderfully pre-
served Trimurti at the
Dieng-complex, Central
Java.

The huge Buddha in
Mendut, hewn from
one single stone. →

A statue at the Singosari-temple, near Malang, East Java.

istic style. So the earliest period of sculpture has been strongly in-
fluenced by the Hindus. Scenes from the Mahabaratha and Ramayana are to be discerned and afterwards the life of Buddha on the famous Borobudur near Jogjakarta. But next to these purely Hindu
reliefs there are also various statues and images carved in stone repre-

70

A richly ornamented temple in Bali, where sculpure has always been among the prominent arts of this paradise island.

senting the everyday-life of the people of that time. These images show us how life was at that time, for wood and bamboo are not endurable and very liable to an early decay.

After the Islam came to Java, the art of sculpture had got into disgrace and gradually it came to a complete standstill. With the intro-

Student of the Academy of Arts at her model

West Irian Liberation Monument in Jakarta

General Sudirman, a fine specimen of present-day sculpture (Jogja Central Java)

duction of the Islam in Java many Hindu-retainers fled to the island of Bali, where they could observe their Hindu religion undisturbedly. So it is no wonder that sculpture in Bali had never disappeared, but has been steadily exercised. And the artistic sense of the Balinese is so great that gates of houses and temples are abundantly decorated. Their material consists of soft stone, which is not very strong and perhaps this might be the never failing encouragement to the Balinese to be always active in this field of art.

During the revolutionary time, however, so about 1944—sculpture was taken at hand again by some artists in Jogja and Solo. At present sculpture is one of the plastic arts taught at the Academy for Plastic Arts in Jogja and in Bandung. In other parts of Indonesia this art came to a complete standstill with the exception of the carving of tomb-stones.

74

METAL WORKS

METAL WORKS

Metalworks were not known until the arrival of the Hindus. But the working of the various metals was not known to all the people of our archipelago. There were districts where the bronze, iron, silver ane gold works were taken over and further developed. In Atjeh tho rentjong, a kind of short dagger is well-kown. The socalled Modjopahit kris is the oldest form of kris (also a kind of dagger) known here in Indonesia. It is more intended as a decoration to the dress than as a weapon. A kris is used to stab the enemy between the shoulder-blades. The later kris is the so-called "pamorkris". This is really intended to be used as a weapon. Krisses are to be found everywhere: in Sumatra, in Java, in Bali as well as in South Sulawesi and in the other islands of Nusa Tenggara such as Lombok, Sumbawa, Timor. Some of them have poisoned blades and therefore rather dangerous. Very rare and beatiful krisses are in the possession of several old families, where they are cherished like precious heirlooms.

*A gold-and silver-smith in his workshop (Makassar,
South Sulawesi).*

Silversmiths of Kota Gedeh (Jogja).

The various forms of krisses depend on the period, in which they were made. In former centuries a mighty sovereign might take a fancy to a kris with a special form and his courtiers were sure to copy it.

The making of bronze objects has disappeared by now, since the Islam was introduced in Java and became more and more influential. In Bali, where the Hindu-retainers had found refuge, the arts of sculpture and the casting of bronze have never had any interruption, so that up to now they are still diligently exercised.

Silver and gold craft is also one of the outstanding features of Indonesian culture. At present the centre for this art is to be found in Java, Bali, Sumatra and Sulawesi. Coming up during the Hindu period, it is but natural that elements of the Hindu-Javanese culture are to be traced in the ornamentation of articles made in Java and Bali. The same motifs are to be seen carved in the walls of the Hindu-

Fine Jogja-silverware for parties.

A fine specimen of a cakeplate of Jogja silverwork.

Mocca-set of Jogja-silver

Silver cup

Smoker's set of copper (Jogja).

Madurese anklets.

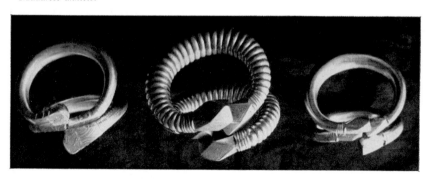

80

Silverworks. Candlestick of Jogja.

Brooch of filigree silverwork,
Makassar.

Javanese temples. In Sumatra and Sulawesi the craftsmen find their inspiration from nature itself: flowers, birds, animals and even ships and houses catch their imagination.

The Indonesian craftsmen hammer, punch and cut their motifs into silver and also spin-cobwebby silver into filigreework. The latter is the special technique applied both in Sumatra and Sulawesi. According to a well-known silversmith at Kota Gedang, Central Sumatra, he was the man who brought this craft of filigreework to Sulawesi, known as Kendari silverworks. In Kendari itself no such craft is known now, which proves that it was indeed introduced by him. At one time a young Dutch controleur (district-officer) bought various articles from him and took them to Holland. When askel what kind of work it was, he could not give any answer but this: "I don't know. I have bought them in Kendari, a small place on the South-eastern peninsula of the Celebes. "And so the name of Kendari-silverwork came into being. At present the centre of this Kendari-silverwork is in Makassar, the

Atjeh filigreework of gold. *Kendari filigree work of gold.*

capital of Sulawesi. It has been further developed by local silversmiths
and many ornaments in gold are made too.

With regard to the Jogja-silverwork, a lump of very hard wax sup-
ports the silver, while the smith punches the motives into the silver,
beginning from the inside of the bowl. Afterwards the bowl is turned
over, with the wax inside, so that the artist can work from the outside.
The back has to be punched deeper, whilst the surface of the relief
is cut. (Embossing-method).

A gold bracelet of Atjeh filigreework.

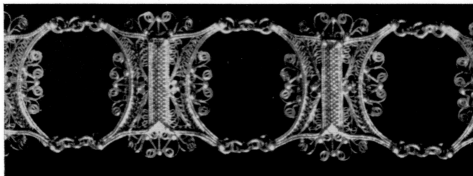

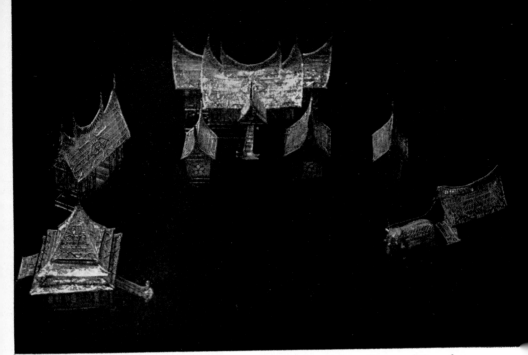

Kota Gedang filigree silverworks, representing a Minangkabau village consisting of an Adat-house with rice-barns, a public hall, a mosque, and a buffalo-drawn cart.

Articles of Balinese silverworks.

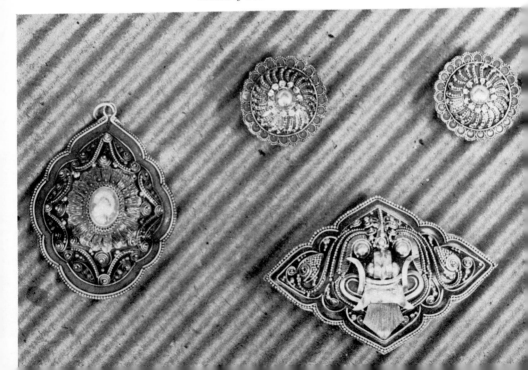

A sirih-set of silver (betel nut)
(Djakarta Museum).

Katjip, instruments to cut the beetlenuts
for the sirih-chewing (18-th century)
Djakarta Museum.

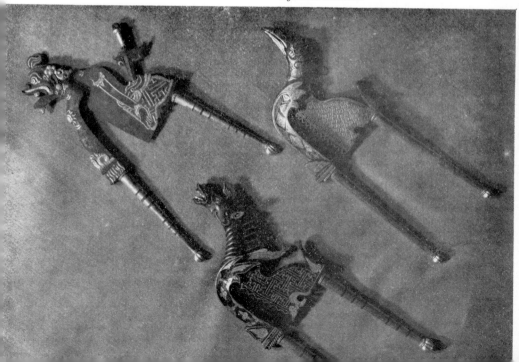

This statue of massive silver is Man-
jushri, one of the three Boddhisatvas,
originating from Amitaba (west). It
is 28 cm high and dates from the 8-th.
century (Djakarta Museum).

p. 86-87:
A curio-shop at PasarBaru, Djakarta.

A silver necklace of the Minangkabau.

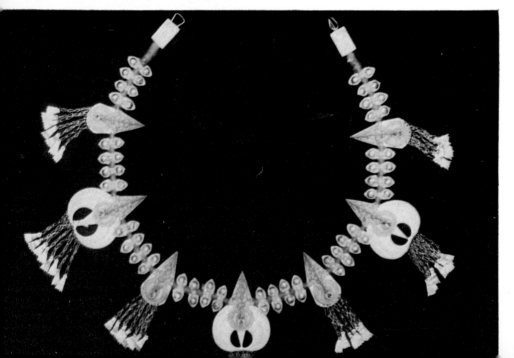

decoration for the completion of Kris (dagger) mainly meant for a sovereign costume. The handles are set with diamonds and other colored stones (Djakarta Museum).

Several types of Balinese Kris. (Kris = dagger). A Balinese kris is as a rule longer than a Javanese one. (Djakarta Museun).

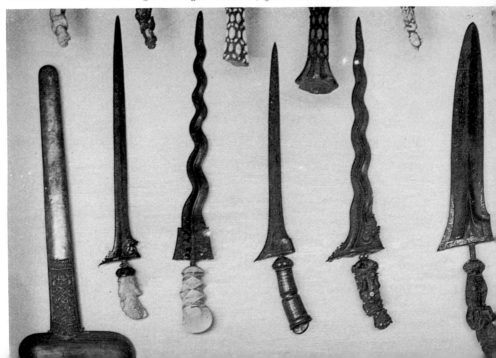

It is amazing to see how many kinds of articles are made and find a ready market everywhere in the world

It should be kept in mind that the ornamentation on articles of the past centuries should have any special meaning. No exact records had been made of those ancient times, at least no details of each ornamentation had ever been described.

In olden times the goldsmiths were employed by the sovereigns and by some of their high courtiers. Wealth, richness and prominence were shown in metals and jewels and the bearers of all this splendour boasted of being the masters of the artisans, which had made the object, which was said to possess special properties throughout the whole country.

So it need not surprise us, that in this intimate house-art gradually and naturally mysticism had come, finding expression in the ornament, so rich with symbolical patterns. The great love, with which the maker had thought and dreamt of, disigned and contemplated his work, the care and the patience, with which he carried it out, that formed the quite ambition, into which mysticism and superstition easily found their way.

But, as gold and silver ornaments came more and more in demand, the number of metal-workers increased. However, independent designers for something really beautiful disappeared and a mere copying of the existing articles caused the decline of their artistic value.

Gradually new forms and designs were made to meet the demands of the time. The gold and silver ornaments are no longer restricted to the use for very special occasions. The women of the 20th century too are fond of wearing these so exotically disigned ornament.

*p. 90-91:   A Minangkabau bridal pair.
The bridegroom wears a kris
an essential part of the whole
attire.*

TIN WORKS

TIN WORKS

Not everybody knows that Indonesia has considerable deposite of tin: it is on the island-groups of Bangka and Billiton, close to the coast of South Sumatra. On these islands the raw tin is extracted from the soil or from the sea by means of dredging and open-cast mining; but it is still more interesting to know something about those industries

A tea-set of tinworks.

which use much of this tin for manufacturing artistic articles to grace many homes.

Artistic tinwork was first taught to the Indonesians by Chinese craftsmen who immigrated here in ancient times and this is probably the reason why many of the original articles manufactured here, mainly consisted of those more suited to the taste of Chinese.

However, little by little, the art sought its inspiration of objects which had an appeal both to Indonesians and Europeans and in this way a new industry was born.

Flower-vases of tin.

Each line follows the other very closely—forming scroll-work without a break or disconnection. Extreme delicasy of touch is needed and the lines are perfectly smooth. The work can only be accomplished slowly and for the artisan, it is a constant strain of the eyesight.

The method of manufacture is extremely simple a rough model is made of the article in shape and this is polished by means of emery powder. Then the work of the artisan really begins as he can now proceed to the chiselling of the designs. The object for decoration is tightly fixed in a clamp, which is held with the toes of the foot. He holds a small chisel in his left hand and a small hammer in the right hand. Then with the chisel and hammer, he marks fine lines on the metal.

At present a new alloy of tin and silver is applied with an amazing effect. Tinwork with this new alloy has a more silvery glow than before and is a real asset for the tea or coffee-table.

LEATHERWORK

LEATHER WORK

The pattern is laid on the hide and the figures copied with a special instrument after which they are cut out. Then it is touched up and polished. Next it is dipped into a mixture of bone-ash and glue-water. Then the puppet, fan or whatever article is made is brought to the dyer, who paints and gilds it, and flattens it between boards padded with thick linen or drill.

The material for the leatherworks of Jogja and Solo is the hide of the water-buffalo. First of all the fresh, wet hide is braced tightly over a bamboo frame and dried in the sun. When it is quite dry, the hair is scraped off with a sharp short knife. Then it is smoked so as to get rid of the remaining fat.

A street-vendor of leather articles in Jogjakarta.

A dalang performs a wayang kulit show (wayang = shadow).

This is a "*gunungan*" (*mountain*) used at the start of a play and at the end of each act. It is carved out of leather and has the shape of a mountain, hence its name "*gunungan*".

The setting-up of a *wayang kulit* show, ready to commence.

101

An exquisitely carved fan of leather.

CERAMICS

Various articles of ceramics.

CERAMICS

The presence of excellent sorts of clay in various parts of Indonesia (Plered near Bandung, Cheribon, Bangka, Purwokerto in Central Java, Malang in East Java, Makassar in South Sulawesi, Saparua in the Moluccas) gave rise to the ceramic industry. In Bandung the Institute of Ceramics has the main task to carry out experiments with various kinds of clay, with several methods of baking, colouring and glazing them. It has a large staff of young engineers trying out the latest methods and mixtures of glazure. Several of them have attended special courses in England in this field. They have a very close contact with the ceramic-producers in the neighbourhood of Baundung. So

104

it's no wonder that the various ceramic factories came into being, producing articles for everyday use, rooftiles, waterpipes, pots and pans for the people, tea-sets, plates, tumblers, ashtrays, flower-pots, vases and so on. This branch of industry has also attracted the attention of several students of arts, who can put into practice their artistic talents. It's amazing to notice the great strides these modern ceramics have made in the last few years. Age-lod articles of use, such as the gendi (jar) in various forms are modelled and painted very attractively. On the island of Bangka they are making porcelain now.

So in this field there is good hope that Indonesia will soon be able to be self-supporting.

Vases for table-lamps, tea-and dinner-sets of ceramics

Modern vases.

THE ART OF PAINTING

THE ART OF PAINTING

During the early part of the 20th century, a few Indonesian painters, of whom the most wellknown was Raden Saleh, acquired considerable fame in the European world of art. But most of the Indonesian art of this period was of an inferior quality and largely of a commercial nature. It was devoted mainly to the painting of Indonesian landscape and imitated Western styles with little originality in concept or design.

In the years preceding World War II, a young group of artists began earnestly to search for new forms of artistic expression and to develop a genuine Indonesian art of universal values and concepts, through the adaptation of modern Western techniques. Many of these young painters formed an association called "Persagi", which included among its founders Sudjojono and the brothers Agus and Otto Djaja. This association, formed before the last World War, started the movement

A Balinese painter at work. He paints in the traditional way.

A modern artist in his atelier.

toward modernisation of Indonesian art, and this trend was later taken up and given added impetus by other art groups, such as the "Pelukis Rakjat" under the leadership of Affandi, and the "Seniman Indonesia Muda". Among the wellknown contemporary artists of Indonesia are Hendra, Henk Ngantung, Emiria Sunasa, Mochtar Apin, Baharuddin, Basuki Resobowo, Sundoro, Trubus, Kartono, Nasroen, Barli, Zaini and Effendi.

In Bali, where the Hindu culture is still predominant, and where the contact with Western civilization has been less intense, these has been quite a different development in art. Up until the 20th century Balinese painting had also developed little since the golden period of the Hindu Empires in the 13th and 14th centuries. It had become stagnant and stereotyped and was still devoted exclusively to the portrayal of Hindu religions scenes and epics. But, in recent years, the painters of Bali have also been brought into contact with Western painting largely, through European painters who have lived and painted in Bali. Under this impact of new ideas and techniques the indigenous

Stranded-
Emiria Sunassa.

Flight-Sudjono

p. 110:
During the revolu-
tionary period many
young artists joined
the guerilla troops.
Their paintings in
that time are mostly
connected with the
guerilla-warfare.
This painting is of
Surono: Frontline.

p. 112:
The fluit-player and
the dancer.

p. 113:
Abducting Sinta.
Yatayu, the vulture
attacks Rahwana,
King of the Raksasa.

Both paintings are
from Agus Djaya.

Balinesse scene: Bathing in the river.

art was rejuvenated and developed into a quite distinctive Balinese style with little of the universal and international concepts of the Indonesian painter elsewhere. The modern Balinese style has an exotic and vigorous quality and while religious concepts are still an integral part of this art, they have become interwoven with everyday aspects of Balinese life. This traditional style does not know time, space nor perspective.

Tjikar, a bull-drawn cart.

This cultural awakening in Indonesia has been further stimulated by the attainment of national independence and the increasing contacts with the modern currents of Western civilisation.

p. 116: Embroidering—Iljas.
p. 117: Ronggeng Deli—Nasroen A.S.

LIST OF CURIO-SHOPS

IN DJAKARTA

Names	*Addresses and phones*
1. Magasin l'Art	71 Tjikini Raya, Gambir 2349.
Sorts of articles:	Jogja, Kendari, Bali, Kota Gedang, Bogor silverworks; Japara, Solo and the Lampongs, Palembang, Silungkang, Balinese woodcarvings; weavings from Timor, Roti, Bali, Batak; batik, scarfs, etc.
2. Indonesian Art and Curios.	63A Tjikini Raya, Gambir 1809.
3. N.V. Luwes	47 Tjikini Raya, Gambir 3705.
Sorts of articles:	Jogja, Kendari, Kota Gedang and Balinese silverworks, Japara and Balinese woodcarvings, and paintings.
4. Jogja-silver Koo	1A Djalan Gondangdia Lama
Sorts of articles:	Specialized in Jogja-silverworks.
5. Arti Warna	10 Djalan Segara III, Gambir 5404.
Sorts of articles:	Specialized in batik, slendangs, scarfs, kelom geulis, small-sized wayang golek puppets, etc.
6. Kota Gedang	8 Djalan Nusantara, Gambir 2031.
Sorts of articles:	Jogja, Kendari, Bali, Kota Gedang and Bogor silverworks, tin-, copper- and leather-works. Japara and Balinese woodcarvings, kris, weavings from the Lampongs, Palembang, Silungkang, Bali, Timor Roti, batik, wickerworks from Tasikmalaya, Bali, Bone, Bogor, Balinese and other Indonesian paintings, etc.
7. Artshop Djawa	2 Djalan Pintu Air, next to Seno.
Sorts of articles:	Jogja-silverworks, etc.
8. Shri Lanka	41 Djalan Pintu Air, Gambir 3498.
Sorts of articles:	Jogja, Kendari, Kota Gedang and Bali silverworks, Japara and Balinese wood-

carvings, plaitingworks from Tasikmalaya, Bali, and Bone;
wayang golek and wayang kulit puppets, Balinese and Javanese masks, weavings from Jogja, Bali, Silungkang, etc.

9. Borobudur
Sorts of articles:

15a Pasar Baru, Gambir 4642.
Jogja, Kendari, Kota Gedang and Bali silverworks,
Japara and Balinese woodcarvings, batik neckties, plaitingworks from Bali, Tasikmalaya, Bone; Silungkang, Timor, Toraja, Palembang, the Lampongs, Batak etc.

10. Toko Djogja
Sorts of articles:

15b Pasar Baru.
Jogja, Kendari, Bali and Kota Gedang silverworks, weavings from the Lampongs, Palembang, Silungkang, Batak; Japara and Balinese woodcarvings, plaitingworks from Bali, Bone and Tasikmalaya etc.

11. Toko Bandung
Sorts of articles:

18c Pasar Baru
Balinese and Japara woodcarvings, Bali, Jogja and Kendari silverworks; etc.

12. Toke Arjuna
Sorts of articles:

16c Djalan Modjopahit
Batik from Jogja, Solo, Tasikmalaya; Jogja; Kendari and Bali silverworks; Balinese and Japara woodcarvings; wayang kulit and wayang golek puppets; plaitingworks from Tasikmalaya and Bali, etc.

13. Toko Garuda
Sorts of articles:

12 Djalan Modjopahit, Batik from Jogja, Solo, Pekalongan; Balinese and Japara woodcarvings; Balinese, Jogja and Kendari silver-works; plaitings works from Tasikmala ya, Bone, Bali; scrafs, leatherworks, Chinese porcelain etc.

119

14.	Toko Oekon	14 Djalan Modjopahit
	Sorts of articles:	Batik from Jogja, Solo and Pekalongan; weavings from Batak, Silungkang and Bali, plaitingworks from Tasikmalaya and Bali etc.
15.	Home Art	41B Djalan Hadji Agus Salim
	Sorts of articles:	Jogja and Balinese silverworks, weavings from Batak, Silungkang and Bali, batik from Jogja and Solo, wayang golek, wayang kulit, Japara and Balinese woodcarvings, paintings etc.
16.	Artshop Banuwati	14 Djalan Nusantara, Gambir 1300
	Sorts of articles:	Specialized in: Bali woodcarvings, paintings, masks; Jogja silverworks, batik etc. Handwork from other parts of Indonesia.
17.	Judith & Wija Wawo Runtu	94 Djalan Hadji Agus Salim; Very selected Balinese woodcarvings, weav-
	Sorts of articles:	ings, silverworks etc.; Jogja batik and silverworks; bamboo-furniture; paintings of Judith Wawo Runtu, Christmas-, bridge-cards etc. etc. painted by Judith Wawo Runtu and antiques.
18.	Wisaya Yasa	10 Djalan Nusantara, Gambir 5293
	Sorts of articles:	Jogja-silverworks.
19.	Fadjar Bhakti Booksellers	22 Djalan Nusantara, Gambir 3264.
	Sorts of articles:	Paintings and books on Indonesia in the Indonesian and English languages, albums with batik-covers etc.
20.	Olislaeger Jewellers	31 Djalan Nusantara, Gambir 1850
	Sorts of articles:	Jogja silvrworks.
21.	The Gold- and Silverhouse	8B Djalan Nusantara.
	Sorts of articles:	Jogja silverworks.
22.	The Souvenirshop	21 Djalan Pembangunan, Gambir 1084
	Sorts of articles:	Jogja and Balinese and Kendari silverworks; Japara and Balinese woodcarvings, weavings from Palembang, Lampong, Silungkang, Batak and Bali; batik from Jogja and Solo and Bandung: etc.

23.	Kemayoran Airport Shop	Kemayoran Airport, Gambir 2500
	Sorts of articles:	Jogja and Balinese silverworks, Japara and Balinese woodcarvings, plaiting-works from Tasikmalaya, Bali and Bone; weavings from Silungkang, Bali and Batak: etc. etc.
24.	Toko Maluku	74 Djalan Menteng Raya, Gambir 1807
	Sorts of articles:	Specialized in batik with ancient and modern designs; ready-made skirts, fancy-pyjamas, dusters, dressing-gowns, table-covers, breakfast-covers of batik.
25.	Sammy	5 Djalan Nusantara Gambir 1532 Balinese woodcarrings.
	Sorts of articles:	

KEBAYORAN

	Prasta-Pandawa	19 Djl. Palatehan I, Blok K/V House of modern Indonesian paintings and arts. Phone: 73297.
	articles:	Paintings.
	Urip Store	40 Djl. Palatehan I. Phone: 72090.
	Sorts of articles:	Balinese woodcarvings, paintings, Nias stone statues etc.

IN BANDUNG

1.	Souvenirshop Tji-hamplelas	37 Djalan Tjihampelas, Phone 2427
	Sorts of articles:	Jogja, Balinese and Kendari silver-works; Japara, Solo and Balinese wood carvings, Toraja and Balinese wicker works, copper and tin and leather-works, original Balinese paintings and weavings, batik and lurik from Jogja and Solo, etc. etc.
2.	N. V. Luwes	40B Djalan Braga, Phone 2257.
	Sorts of articles:	Jogja, Balinese and Kendari silverworks, Japara and Balinese woodcarvings, Toraja and Balinese wickerworks weavings from the Lampong, Palembang,

		Silungkang, Timor, Bali, Batak, Toraja; paintings etc.
3.	Artshop Tatarah	51C Djalan Braga
	Sorts of articles:	Paintings, Balinese woodcarvings etc.
4.	Sin Sin	47 Djalan Braga
	Sorts of articles:	Jogja silverworks, copper and leatherworks, Balinese woodcarvings etc.
5.	Toko Kelom Geulis Keng	21 Djalan Patjinan Lama
	Sorts of articles:	Specialized in wooden cloques.
6.	Ceramic Factory Tjipaganti	136 Djalan Tjipaganti, Phone 8318.
	Shop	64C Djalan Braga (1st floor)
		Specialized in lovery ceramics, own designs.
7.	Mulan	64 Djalan Asia-Afrika, Phone 4606
	Sorts of articles:	Specialized in lovely ceramics, bamboo articles (lamp-shades etc.) handicrafts etc.
8.	M. Sukama	62 Djalan Braga, Phone 3808.
	Sorts of articles:	Ceramics, wayang golek puppets, baskets from Tasikmalaya and Bone, etc.
9.	Wisaya Yasa	42B Djalan Braga
	Sorts of articles:	Jogja silverworks.
10.	Giftshop Edina	Djalan Atjeh
	Sorts of articles:	Balinese and Japara woodcarvings, paintings, etc.
11.	Giftshop Agam	5 Djalan Dago
		Specialized in batik kains and batik ready-made clothes.
12.	Ramayana	48 Djalan Braga
	Sorts of articles:	Jogja silverworks.
13.	Kebangkitan	30 Djalan Bandjaran, Phone 4721.
	Sorts of articles:	Modern cloques, Madjalaya weavings, Tasikmalaya plaitingworks, hats, umbrellas etc.
	Main Office: Kebangkitan	52A Djalan Mamandjaya, Tasikmalaya.

IN SURABAYA:

Along Tundjungan there are various large shops with all sorts of articles and also at the numerous hotels.

IN MAKASSAR:

1. Toko Keradjinan   20 Djalan Somba Opu
   Sorts of articles: Weavingsworks from Toraja, baskets from Bone and Takalar, woodcarvings from Toraja etc.
2. Minasabadji   46 Djalan Somba Opu
   Sorts of articles: Baskets from Bone, woodcarvings and weaving from Toraja etc.
3. Toko Mutiara   1117A Djalan Somba Opu
   Sorts of articles: Weavings and baskets from Toraja etc.
4. M. Thahir
   Sorts of articles: Kendari silverfiligree.
5. Kong Sing   15 Djalan Klenteng
   Sorts of articles: Kendari silverworks.
6. Wing Tjing   37 Djalan Klenteng
   Sorts of articles: Kendari silverworks.

IN BALI:

1. Craftshouse Rama   Titihstreet—Den Pasar
   Sorts of articles: Famous Bratan's silverworks and woodcarvings.
2. Curiosity Shop of Mas   Mas village.
   Sorts of articles: Exclusive woodcarvings of Mas.
3. Art Gallery Rodja   Mas village.
   Sorts of articles: Woodcarvings, weavings, paintings.
4. Toko Surja   Tjeluk
   Sorts of articles: Balinese silver and goldworks.
5. Toko Gana   Klungkung
   Sorts of articles: Woodcarvings, beautiful weavings of gold and silver, silverworks (bowls and plates), plaited works (food-covers, hats).
6. Toko Kresna   Klungkung
   Sorts of articles: Antiquities, curiosities and woodcarvings.
7. Toko Indra   Klungkung
   Sorts of articles: Antiquities, curiosities and woodcarvings.
8. Toko Keradjinan   Klungkung
   Sorts of articles: Antiquities, curiosities and woodcarvings.

9.	Toko Artja	Marketstreet—Den Pasar
	Sorts of articles:	Silveroworks, curiosities and woodcarvings.
10.	Toko Sudimampir	36 Marketstreet—Den Pasar
	Sorts of articles:	Curiosities, woodcarvings, silverworks.
11.	Toko Abdullah	38 Marketstreet—Den Pasar
	Sorts of articles:	Antiquities, curiosities and woodcarvings.
12.	Batuan	Batuan, Sukawati
	Sorts of articles:	Woodcarvings of Batuan. Tjeluk, Gianjar Silverworks.
13.	Toko Klungkung	Marketstreet—Den Pasar Belaluan—Den Pasar
	Sorts of articles:	Balinese articles of art and curies.
14.	Toko Oka	Djalan Ngura Rai—Den Pasar Belaluan—Den Pasar
	Sorts of articles:	Beautiful weavings, exclusive woodcarvings, all sorts of silverworks, plaiting works and paintings.
15.	Toko Eutji	Djalan Ngura Rai—Den Pasar
	Sorts of articles:	Woodcarvings, weavings and paintings
16.	Jajasan Keradjinan Bali (Bali Art Foundation)	Djalan Museum—Den Pasar
	Sorts of articles:	Woodcarvings, silverworks, weavings and paintings.
17.	The Painter's Society of Ubud	Ubud
	Sorts of articles:	Balinese paintings.

IN SUMATERA:

Palembang:

Along the Djalan Djendral Sudirman are several shops where Palembang songkets (gold and silver weavings) and other weavings from the Lampongs can be had.

Bukittinggi:

1. Toko Ramona 12 Djalan Tionghoa—phone: 296 Kain
   Sorts of articles: balapak weaving of Pandai Sikat, kain Silungkang, Kota Gedang filigree-silverworks.

Medan:

1. Toko Djawa   Kesawan
   Sorts of articles: Copperworks, Kota Gedang filigree-silverworks, weavings from the Batak-lands, Silungkang and the Lampongs, Balinese woodcarvings, weavings, Jogja silverworks and batik.

2. Toko Nauli   Djalan Perdana
   Sorts of articles: Copperworks, Kota Gedang filigree-silverworks, weavings from the Batak-lands, Silungkang and the Lampongs.

3. Begeer van Kempen   Djalan Istana
   & Vos
   Sorts of articles: Specialized in Jogja-silverworks.

Brastagi:
Modesty Souvenir-shop
Sorts of articles: Weaving from all parts of Indonesia, woodcarvings, basket-works, carved bamboo, filigree-works, Batak antiquities.

A Japara craftsman at work.

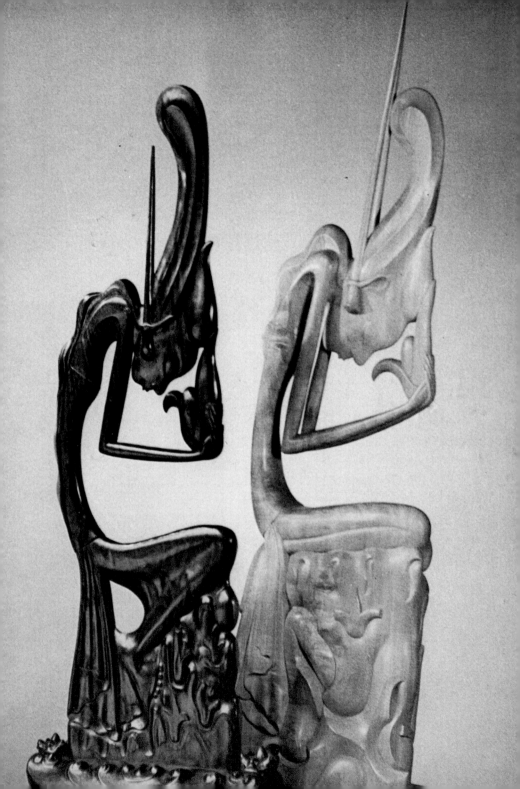

Contents

Back cover:
The "topeng" (masks) are used during
performing a "Topeng"-dance. The dance
itself relects fragments from Javanese history.